CLYDE
The Never-Give-Up Horse

Copyright © 2016 Deborah Young

All rights reserved. This book or any portion thereof may not be reproduced or used in any manner whatsoever without the express written permission of the author, except for the use of brief quotations in a book review.

Photography by Karen Clevely, Anna Hill and Stephen Legendre

Layout by Pattie Steib

ISBN-13: 978-1539824701
ISBN-10: 1539824705

Printed in the United States of America

First Edition, December 2016
10 9 8 7 6 5 4 3 2 1

This book is dedicated to all who struggle with the problems that life throws at them. Never give up and never settle for less than your dreams.

ACKNOWLEDGMENTS

The author would like to acknowledge all the people who helped to tell Clyde's story.

A special thanks to the real Bonny and Clyde who made this book possible.

CLYDE
The Never-Give-Up Horse

Written By
Deborah Young

In Saskatchewan, Canada, there was a farmer who had a small herd of Clydesdale horses.

Each year the farmer had beautiful foals. Then one day the farmer fell on hard times.

He could no longer feed his horses. He was sad because he knew all of his horses would have to find new homes.

People saw the pictures of the horses on the online adoption site. Each day another horse left the farm.

Soon the farmer could no longer buy feed and hay. The horses became thin and sickly.

Finally there was only one left, a yearling colt that had not eaten for so long he was skin and bones.

No one wanted the colt because he was the only one that was different from the rest.

The little lone colt wasn't bay like the others. No one wanted a black Clydesdale.

Far away in Louisiana, Bonny was looking at the adoption site. She did not intend to buy another horse. There was the photo of a black colt named Nick.

Two more days - that is all he had left to be adopted. She looked in his eyes, and something told her he was worth saving.

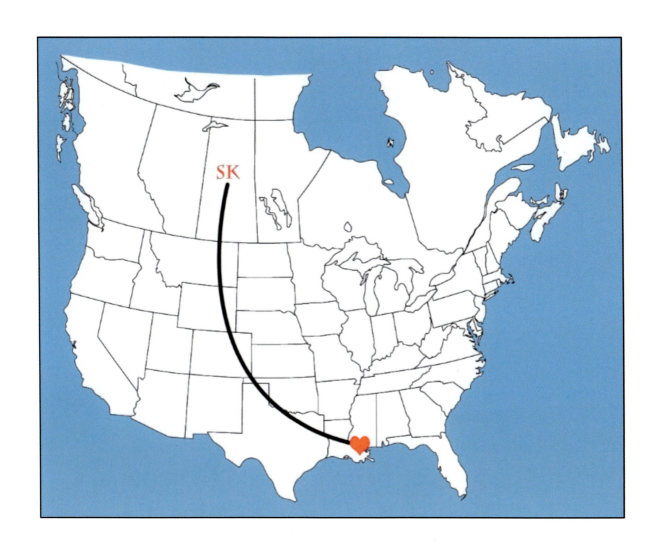

Bonny called the adoption agency.
Yes, the little black colt was still available. She bought him right away and made plans to have him sent to her home. Now from Canada he was headed to his last home in Louisiana.

The colt had never been touched by a person. He did not know where he was going and everything frightened him on his long trip to his new home in Louisiana.

Bonny was waiting for him to arrive. She had a stall ready for him with plenty of soft shavings and fresh hay.

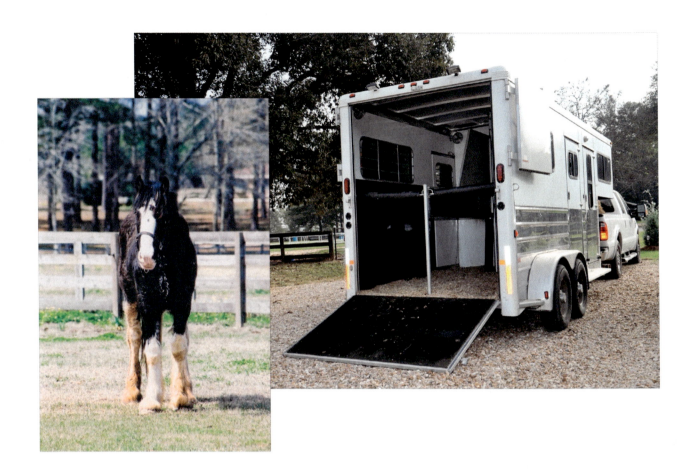

Clyde had just arrived at the farm. He was still dirty and worn out from his long trip.

Bonny took one look at him when he walked off the trailer and said, "You are not a Nick. From now on you will be my Clyde."

It took many weeks for Clyde to start feeling better. Finally he was kicking up his heels, galloping, and playing in the pasture.

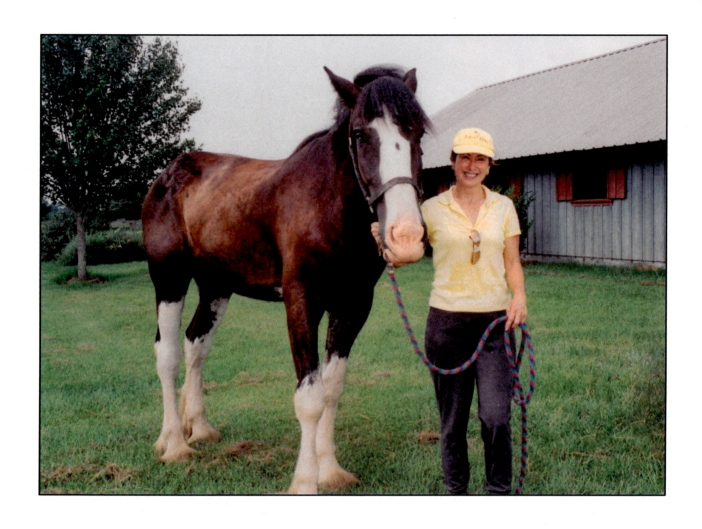

Even after six months, he was still a thin guy that was still growing. Bonny knew he would need good food and special care to become a full-sized Clydesdale horse.

Soon it was Clyde's first birthday. He had a special party and invited all his friends.

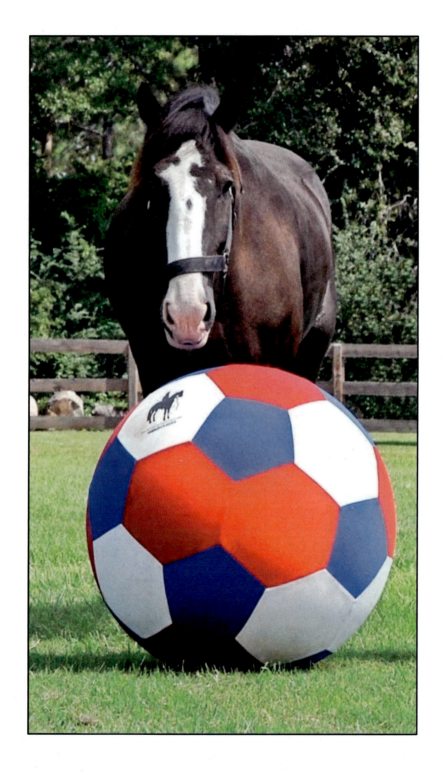

As Clyde began to adjust to his new home, he found out he was no longer afraid.

Bonny started teaching him tricks and he learned quickly. With Bonny's care, he knew he would never give up his dream of helping others, just like Bonny helped him.

Clyde learned so many tricks that people asked him to perform at special charity events.

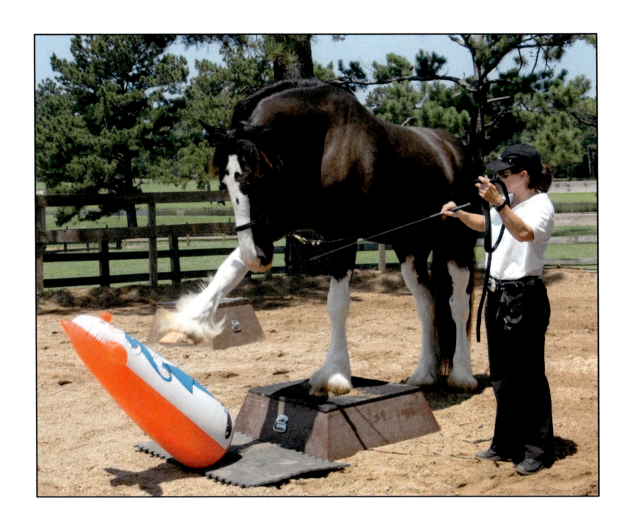

Clyde wanted to be the only boxing Clydesdale in Louisiana. Just like Rocky in the movie, he wanted to show people what they can do if they never give up.

Clyde was invited to be a part of the St. Jude's Children's Research Hospital's Dream Day Foundation. The Fishin' Galore event in Clinton, Louisiana, is such a special time for these children. The sick children showed Clyde how brave they were. They were the ones fighting the biggest fight of all: Cancer.

It might have been St. Jude's "Fishin' Galore," but everywhere there were Smiles Galore, too.

Clyde made sure of that.

The next year Clyde was so happy when he was asked to be a part of Special Olympics. He remembered when he was young and afraid. He knew he could make the children feel brave.

The children dipped their hands in special paint and made a wish they hoped would come true.

Later, Clyde learned that some of the children at his events are adopted just like him. He knew what it was like becoming part of a new family. Bonny's love and care showed him how his own kindness would make the children happy. Clyde knew just like him, they are all picked from the heart.

Everywhere he goes people applaud his tricks and his way of putting smiles on the faces of sick children. The more attention he gets, the harder he tries and the more people love him. He is no longer the little colt no one would buy because he was the wrong color.

Bonny knows how lucky she is to have a horse like Clyde. Clyde's friends may be sick or disabled. But, Clyde's kisses are all the same.

Bonny never turned her back on the black colt who needed a new home. Clyde never turns his back on anyone that needs his help. He is determined to be strong. He will never give up because his friends expect that from him.

Facts About Clydesdales

1. Horses are measured in hands. A hand equals four inches.
2. Clydesdales stand 16 to 18 hands and can weigh 2,000 pounds.
3. Most Clydesdales are bay but other colors are brown, black, roan, and chestnut.
4. They also have white legs with long hair known as feathers. Most have a large white blaze on their faces.
5. Their horseshoes are the size of dinner plates.
6. Clydesdales originated in Scotland.
7. Clydesdales have been used in farming for hundreds of years. They were also used as war horses during the Middle Ages.
8. They are known for their good disposition, intelligence, and willingness to learn.
9. Clydesdales have been put on the rare breeds list with less than 5,000 horses worldwide.
10. Clydesdales are best known today as the six horse hitch of Anheuser Busch Company of St. Louis, Missouri. These teams tour not only the United States but the world.

Clyde's Education Page

1. What measurement is used to measure horses?_____
2. How many inches is the measurement?_____
3. What color are most Clydesdales?_____
4. What color is Clyde?_____
5. Where was Clyde born?_____
6. What was Clyde's name on the adoption site?_____
7. How many days did Clyde have left to be adopted?_____
8. What kind of soft bedding was in Clyde's stall. _____
9. How many pounds can a Clydesdale weigh?_____
10. What is the long hair on their legs called? _____
11. What country were Clydesdales originally found? _____
12. In what state does Clyde live?_____
13. How many horses are in the Clydesdale hitch?_____
14. What is the white marking on their face called?_____
15. Their shoes are the size of what kitchen item?_____

Words to Know

Bay- Reddish brown coat with black points. Mane, tail, legs, muzzle, and tips of their ears are black points.

Black- Black coat color with black mane and tail.

Blaze- a white stripe running down the face of an animal.

Chestnut- red hair coat with mane and tail the same color.

Feathers- long hair on the lower leg of Clydesdales. Feathers can also be found on other breeds of horses.

Middle Ages- A period in European history from the 1100 to 1400.

Roan- white hairs mixed with another body color such as black, bay, or chestnut.

Scotland- Country in the northern part of the United Kingdom.

The Rest of Clyde's Story...

This story about a skinny, black Clydesdale colt in Saskatchewan, Canada, is true. Bonny really did see a photo of him on an adoption site and did buy him sight unseen. Yes, he really did have two more days before he was going to be shipped off to the auctions. Clyde would have ended up at a feed lot to be fattened up for horse meat.

Clyde's mother was a PMU mare bred to produce pregnant mare urine that is used in hormone replacement for women. The foals were a necessary by-product because without pregnant mares, there is no pregnant mare urine to be collected and sold. The foals were the necessary result of the operation but they were "throw aways." The plan was to get them sold as soon as they were weaned, their dams pregnant again, and start the cycle all over. When the demand for the urine collapsed, the foals and remaining mares were put on a website to be adopted.

Contrary to popular belief adopted horses are not free. Clyde's purchase price from the adoption group was $750. Shipping costs to have him transported to Folsom, Louisiana, was another $1,800. Clyde's total cost was $2,550 but this did not include vaccinations and general health checkups after he arrived.

Clyde was sent to Bonny as a wild, unhandled colt that was scared of everything and everyone. When she saw him come off the trailer she wondered, "What in the world was I thinking?"

Fortunately, it did not take long for Clyde to come around and start to bond with Bonny and become her companion.

He had to learn basic horse skills, being led and tied, allowing people to brush him, and picking up his feet for the farrier. He learned these things very quickly and became an important part of Carousel Farm. He was soon a very different horse from the wild baby that had been herded off the trailer.

As time passed, Bonny saw he was a real ham for attention. It was easy to teach Clyde little tricks because he was so happy to please Bonny. As the tricks became more advanced, Bonny began to see that Clyde was not a timid rescue any more but a horse that loved to be around people and perform for them. She knew he could put smiles on the faces of people, no matter where he traveled.

Word began to spread about Clyde, the trick horse. Requests came in for Bonny and Clyde to perform at fundraisers and charity events. All the spectators saw was this happy horse doing tricks and giving kisses to sick children. Most did not know Clyde's real story.

In the end, this is the story of a horse that didn't have a future and a horse woman who decided to take a chance. Clyde hopes that all the people who hear his story will never give up searching for their own place in the world and making their own dreams come true.

ABOUT THE AUTHOR

    If you talk to the author's mother, she will swear her daughter's first word was "Momma" and the second word was "horse." Deborah Young grew up on a large farm in North Missouri where her family raised corn, soybeans, cattle, and hogs. In 1964, she won her first pony in a contest at the county fair. Pony, the perfect Shetland pony, along with her larger pony, Dusty, carried her to many wins at horse shows and 4-H events.

    Deborah graduated from Northeast Missouri State University, now known as Truman State University, with a degree in English education and a minor in library science.

    Her husband was transferred to New Orleans in 1975. In 1977, she answered an ad in the Times Picayune and purchased AM Golden Caroler, a purebred Arabian gelding. Charlie was a once-in-a-lifetime horse and fueled her love for Arabian horses. Although she loved Arabians, she decided to go back to her pony roots. In 1997, she bought a Dartmoor mare from Farnley Farms at White Post, Virginia and imported a stallion from Shilstone Rocks Stud in England.

    Dartmoors are a British Native pony and are on the rare breeds list. There are less than 400 Dartmoors in the United States. For many years, she and her husband attended expos around the country so people could learn more about this rare breed.

    After being a school librarian for 38 years, the author decided it was time to get serious about her own writing. Clyde The-Never-Give-Up-Horse is her first book. Readers will be happy to know they just might find a new horse or pony galloping into her next story.

Made in the USA
Monee, IL
27 September 2022

14589562R00026